TRANSPORT

Nicola Barber

WAYLAND

First published in 2010 by Wayland

Copyright © Wayland 2010

Wayland
338 Euston Road
London NW1 3BH

Wayland Australia
Level 17/207 Kent Street
Sydney NSW 2000

Series Editor: Nicola Edwards
Series Consultant: Annette Trolle
Designer: Jane Hawkins
Picture Researcher: Kathy Lockley

British Library Cataloguing in Publication Data
Barber, Nicola.
   Viking life.
   Transport.
   1. Vikings--Transportation--Juvenile literature.
   2. Viking ships--Juvenile literature.
   I. Title
   388'.089395-dc22

ISBN: 978 0 7502 6386 3

Picture acknowledgements
The Art Archive/Historiska Muséet, Oslo/Alfredo Dagli Orti: 14; The Art
Gallery Collection/Alamy: 15; Bernie Epstein/Alamy: 11; Bibliotheque
des Arts Decoratifs, Paris, France/Archives Charmet/Bridgeman Art Library, London: 17; Bymuseum, Oslo,
Norway/Index/Bridgeman Art Library, London: 8, 29; Werner Forman Archive/Bergen Maritime Museum: 27;
Werner Forman Archive/National Museum, Copenhagen: 4, 19; Werner Forman Archive/University Museum of
National Antiquities, Uppsala, Sweden: 18; Hemis/Alamy: 13; INTERFOTO/Alamy: 6, 28; Lennart Larsen,
National Museum of Denmark: 22; © Museum of Cultural History, University of Oslo/Eirik Irgens Johnsen: 25;
Museum of National Antiquities, Stockholm, Sweden: title page, 20; iStockphoto 26; Shutterstock/ COVER
(main), 7, 10, 12; Ian Thompson: 9; © 2005 TopFoto/TopFoto.co.uk: COVER (inset), 23; North Wind Picture
Archives/Alamy: 16; © York Archaeological Trust: 24; Anna Yu/Alamy: 21

The author and publisher would like to thank Torkild Waagaard for his kind permission to reproduce his
artwork of a Viking helmet on the panels in this book

Printed in China

Wayland is a division of Hachette Children's Books, an Hachette UK company.

www.hachette.co.uk

Contents

Words in **bold** can be found in the glossary.

The Viking world

The Vikings came from Scandinavia, the region of northern Europe that is made up of modern-day Denmark, Norway and Sweden. From the 8th to the 11th centuries, many Vikings left their homelands on journeys of piracy, discovery and **commerce**. This time is often called the 'Viking Age'.

←

This stone carving from Sweden shows a typical Viking ship. It is double-ended and has a square sail.

Raiders, explorers and traders

The word Viking comes from the **Old Norse** language, meaning 'pirate', or 'piracy'. For around 300 years, the Vikings were the most skilled boat-builders and seamen in northern Europe. They used their skills to sail across seas and up rivers, raiding and **plundering** as they went. From the earliest raids in the 8th century, the sight of Viking ships on the horizon was enough to spark fear and panic in communities across Europe. The Vikings attacked places in the British Isles, France and even as far south as Spain and Africa.

→

This is a modern-day interpretation of a Viking longship **prow** decoration. The Vikings added carved dragon heads to the prows of their longships as they believed these would protect the crews against sea monsters.

Not all Vikings were pirates or **raiders**. They were also explorers and **colonizers**, sailing west to Iceland, Greenland and even as far as North America. The Vikings were great traders, too. Many Vikings from Sweden travelled eastwards along rivers that led them deep inland, to trade for goods from distant lands.

Travel at home

While many Vikings set out on exciting voyages, others remained in their Scandinavian homeland. The Viking people of Scandinavia were farmers and fishers. They built different kinds of boats for carrying **cargo**, for ferrying people across narrow stretches of water, and for fishing. In the winter, they travelled across the snowy Scandinavian landscape on skis and skates, and hauled loads on sledges.

A Viking Object

The prow of the Svea Viking, a reconstruction Viking ship that was used for tourist cruises around Stockholm in Sweden. The prow is the front end of the ship (see page 10). The Vikings often decorated the prows of their longships with fiercesome carved heads. It is likely that these decorated prows were removed and stored when the ships were at sea. They were replaced as the ship neared land.

Sea routes

Vikings from different parts of Scandinavia travelled in different directions from their homeland. Vikings from Norway set out westwards on voyages across the North Sea. The Danish Vikings also sailed west to attack England and the coast of France.

Viking raids

The first recorded Viking raid on England was on the **monastery** of Lindisfarne, in the northeast of England, in 793. This was the first of many hit-and-run raids on wealthy monasteries in England, Scotland and Ireland. Small bands of Vikings relied on surprise, and the fact that the monasteries were largely undefended, to make their attacks. They plundered the monasteries for treasure, and they captured prisoners to be kept or sold as slaves.

This medieval illustration, painted after the Viking Age ended, shows a Viking fleet approaching land.

The Vikings also sailed down the French coast, plundering as they went. Some Viking raiders ventured as far as Spain, and a few even sailed into the Mediterranean Sea.

Settlers and explorers

Not all Viking voyages were for raiding and plundering. From the 870s onwards, thousands of Vikings made the perilous sea voyage from Scandinavia to Iceland to start new lives on the island. The Vikings also established settlements in Greenland. They even explored North America, although attempts to set up a **colony** there were quickly abandoned.

➡ This map shows how far the Vikings travelled across seas and along rivers on their raiding and trading expeditions.

Island stops

The Vikings from Norway used the islands in the North Sea as stepping-stones to Britain and Ireland. The Faroes, Shetland and Orkney islands were about two days' sailing time from the coast of Norway. The Vikings settled on these islands, on the Hebrides off the west coast of Scotland, and on the Isle of Man in the Irish Sea. These island bases provided ideal starting points for raids on Scotland, Ireland and Wales.

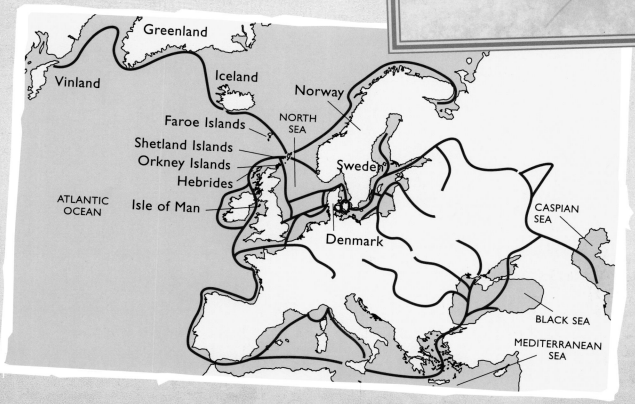

Greenland

Vinland

Iceland

Norway

Faroe Islands

NORTH SEA

Shetland Islands

Orkney Islands

Sweden

Hebrides

ATLANTIC OCEAN

Isle of Man

CASPIAN SEA

Denmark

BLACK SEA

MEDITERRANEAN SEA

Viking longships

The kind of ships built by the Vikings for sea voyages and battles were known as longships. These long, narrow ships were decorated at the front (prow) with a carving of an animal – often a dragon or a snake.

↑ The Sea Stallion from Glendalough is a reconstruction of the longship shown in the picture opposite. It is the biggest reconstructed Viking ship in the world.

Wooden ships

Longships were built out of planks of wood – usually oak. Each long plank was shaped, and then overlapped and fastened to the next plank with nails. Any gaps between the planks were filled with tarred wool and animal hair to make the ship watertight. A longship was strong, flexible and light – and it cut through the water very fast. It was also shallow, so it could easily be pulled up on to a beach, or rowed down a river.

Oars and sail

Longships were powered by oars. The oars fitted through holes along the side of the ship. Large ships had crews of about 60 men. On long voyages they took turns to row. There were no seats, so the oarsmen sat on storage chests which were filled with everything needed for the expedition.

There was also a mast for hoisting a square-shaped sail. If the wind was blowing in the right direction, the sail helped to power the longship through the water. It's likely that sails were made from wool, criss-crossed with leather to help keep them in shape when they got wet.

A Viking Object

Only about a quarter of this great longship survives, but **archaeologists** have pieced it together to give an idea of the size of the ship. The ship was built from oak, in Ireland. It had 60 oars and a crew of between 60 and 70 men. The long, narrow shape meant that the ship could move at great speed through the water.

➡

The remains of one of the longships found in Roskilde Fjord in Denmark. The ship was built in Dublin, Ireland, in around 1042.

Other ships

As well as longships, the Vikings built many other different kinds of ship. All of these ships were made from wood, and most were built in roughly the same way as the longship.

Cargo ships

The ships built by the Vikings for carrying cargo were wider, deeper and slower than the sleek, narrow longships. These cargo ships were called *knarrs*. They had fewer oars than a longship – the weight of the cargo made it difficult for oarsmen to power a *knarr* along.

The oars were used mostly to **manoeuvre** the ship in and out of landing places. Out at sea, the Viking sailors relied on wind power. A *knarr* had a taller mast and a bigger sail than a longship.

 At the Viking Ship Museum in Roskilde, Denmark, boat-builders have reconstructed many different types of Viking boat, including the two shown here.

Knarrs were built to take heavy loads, and they had to be strong to withstand stormy seas and rough weather. Cargo such as **timber**, cloth or wool was packed into an open space in the centre of the ship. In rough weather, the cargo was tied down and covered with animal skins to keep it safe. These sturdy ships were also used by the Vikings for voyages of exploration, and for transporting families, their **livestock** and belongings across the seas to settle in new places.

Small boats

The Vikings made small boats for many different uses. There were ferries for carrying passengers across **fjords** and narrow rivers. Small rowing boats were used for fishing. There were even small, four-oared boats that were carried on board, or towed behind, bigger ships such as *knarrs*.

A boat-building scene from the Bayeux Tapestry.

A Viking Object

The Bayeux Tapestry was made to record the conquest of England in 1066 by William, Duke of Normandy (William the Conqueror). The Normans were descended from Vikings who had settled in this part of France, so we can be fairly certain that the Normans used similar practices to the Vikings to build their boats. Here, the boatbuilders are working with axes to trim the planks used to make the ships.

Life at sea

The Vikings' ships were sturdy and seaworthy, but there was no shelter on board. Life at sea was hard. For this reason, the Vikings avoided making voyages during the stormy winter months.

Getting some sleep

If it was possible to do so, the Vikings sailed along a coastline so that they could stop and go ashore at night. They pulled their ships up on to land, then set up tents made of wool for shelter. But on long voyages across seas and oceans this was not possible. The crew had to sleep on deck, wherever they could find a space. They set up tents and huddled under blankets, or in sleeping bags made from animal skins.

Finding the way

The Vikings did not have any maps, but they had many different ways of working out where they were. They knew which landmarks to look out for when they were in sight of a coast. Far out at sea, they used the position of the sun in the sky during the day, and the stars at night, to find their way.

A weather vane such as this swung from the prow of a Viking ship to indicate the direction of the wind.

The direction of the waves, and even the type of wildife around was all useful information to Viking sailors. All of this knowledge was passed down from generation to generation.

Eating and drinking

For long voyages, ships were loaded up with supplies of fresh water and food. Water was stored in animal skins. The Vikings also had beer to drink. Food included dried or salted fish and bread, cheese and apples. There is some evidence that the Vikings also took live animals on board for food. When it was possible, they lit a cooking fire on deck to produce hot, fresh food.

➡

This painting imagines the moment when Leif Eriksson sighted land on his journey to North America.

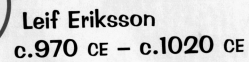

Leif Eriksson
c.970 CE – c.1020 CE

Leif Eriksson was the son of Erik the Red, the Viking who set up settlements in Greenland. From a Viking called Bjarni Herjolfsson, Leif heard tales of a land far to the west of Greenland. Bjarni had glimpsed this land after becoming lost in thick fog on his way from Iceland to Greenland. Leif decided to retrace Bjarni's journey.

Using Bjarni's descriptions of what he had seen, Leif and his crew worked their way back along Bjarni's route. They eventually made landfall in North America at a place they named Vinland (Vine-land). They spent the winter there before returning to Greenland. Leif never went back to Vinland.

River transport

As well as crossing the seas, the Vikings also sailed and rowed their ships up rivers. Some of these river journeys were for raiding, others were for trading.

River raids

When the Vikings first started their raids, they attacked places that lay along coastlines. But the Viking longships were shallow enough to travel up rivers. As they grew more bold, the Vikings began to launch attacks on settlements far inland. In Ireland, the Vikings began to raid monasteries along rivers in the 830s. In France, Viking longships sailed up the Seine in the north, the Loire in the west and the Garonne in the south. Paris was attacked by a Viking army in 845, and again in 885, when around 700 longships made their way up the river Seine.

The Vikings attack Paris in 885. A huge Viking army sailed up the Seine in 700 longships.

River trade

Other Vikings, mostly from Sweden, were more interested in trading. From the Baltic Sea they rowed and sailed upstream deep into the Russian continent. The Russian rivers were full of rocks and **rapids**. The Vikings often had to manhandle their boats around these obstacles. When they reached the end of these rivers, they hauled their ships out of the water. They carried them, or rolled them on logs, until they reached other rivers such as the Dniepr or the Volga.

The Dniepr took the Vikings to the Black Sea, from where they could reach the city of Constantinople (modern-day Istanbul), capital of the **Byzantine Empire**. The Volga led into the Caspian Sea, and to trade routes leading to Baghdad, at the heart of the **Islamic** world.

For long river journeys, the Vikings probably used boats rather like **dugout** canoes, which could be carried overland.

Written at the time

In his book *De Administrando Imperio* the Byzantine emperor Constantine II described how the Vikings (the 'Rus') worked their boats around dangerous places in the river Dniepr:

'… in the middle of [the river] are high rocks… Against these, then, comes the water and wells up and dashes down over the other side, with a mighty and terrific din. Therefore the Rus do not venture to pass between them, but put in to the bank hard by [nearby], disembarking the men on to dry land, but leaving the goods on board; they then strip and go back into the water, feeling with their feet to avoid striking on a rock… They work forward with poles, some at the prow [front], some amidships, others in the stern [back]; and with all this careful procedure they … edge round under the river-bank.'

Trade networks

Viking trade networks extended far and wide. Goods were transported vast distances by sea, river and over land.

↑ These scales come from Birka (see pages 20–1). They would have been used by a trader to weigh silver for payment.

Silver coins

Silver was very important to the Vikings. Jewellery made from silver showed off a person's wealth and **status**. The Vikings **imported** huge numbers of Arab silver coins, but they were not interested in them as money. The heavier the coin, the more silver it contained and the more valuable it was. The Vikings melted down the coins and used the silver to make jewellery.

Spices, silk and glass

Other valuable imports were spices and silk. These came from China and other far away places, often via the Byzantine Empire. Spices were used to flavour food. Silk for trimming clothes was a luxury that only wealthy Vikings could afford.

Pieces of glass were another major import. The glass was used to make beautiful beads. Beads were extremely popular amongst Viking women. Like silver, wearing beads showed off a person's wealth and status.

Viking exports

The Vikings had a rich supply of goods that they could take from their homelands as **exports**. Warm furs, walrus ivory for carving, the skins of walruses for making strong ropes, iron and timber, and **whetstones** used to sharpen knives all came from Scandinavia. **Amber** was another valuable item. Found around the shores of the Baltic Sea, this **fossilized resin** was highly prized for its deep yellow-orange colour and its smoothness.

Other items included honey, wax and weapons. The Vikings were also slave-traders. Men and women were captured during raids, then sold on to Arab merchants in exchange for silver.

➡

This amber chess piece comes from Denmark.

A Viking Object

This chess piece is made out of amber. It may represent Thor, the Viking god of thunder. Amber was washed up on the North Sea and Baltic Sea beaches, where it was collected by the Vikings. The Vikings used amber to make pendants, finger rings, spindle whorls, and gaming pieces like this one.

Birka: a trading centre

As trade developed in the Viking world, some towns in Scandinavia became important trading centres. One of these was Birka in modern-day Sweden.

↑ Some of the objects found during excavations at Birka.

Summer and winter

Birka lay at the northern end of Bjorko (Birch Island), in Lake Malar. It provided a safe harbour for ships carrying goods from other parts of Scandinavia, and from the east. In summer it was reached by ship, but in winter the sea froze over. Then, merchants brought their furs on sledges across the ice.

Grave evidence

We know a lot about Birka from **archaeological excavations** of graves in the town. Many fine fur cloaks have been uncovered in graves, showing how important the fur trade was for the town.

Written at the time

A Christian monk and **missionary** called Ansgar visited Birka for the first time in 829. In his book, the *Life of Ansgar*, Bishop Rimbert wrote about the perils of travel experienced by the monk and his followers:

The merchants with whom they were travelling defended themselves vigorously and for a time successfully, but eventually they were conquered and overcome by the pirates, who took from them their ships and all that they possessed, whilst they themselves barely escaped on foot to land… With great difficulty they accomplished their long journey … and eventually arrived at the Swedish port called Birka.'

Other luxury items include silks and fine cloths such as **brocade**, which were imported from the east. Many traders' scales (see page 18) have been found in the town. These were used for weighing out silver.

Well-defended town

So many ships sailed into Birka that it had no fewer than three harbours. Such a thriving and wealthy trading centre needed to be well-defended. The town had a small fort, and it was enclosed by an earthen **rampart**. It is likely that there were wooden lookout towers at intervals along the rampart.

The doors of a chapel dedicated to Ansgar, on Bjorko (Birch Island), are decorated with scenes from his travels.

Land transport

Travel over land was not easy in much of Scandinavia during the Viking Age. Roads were often little more than muddy tracks. Forests, marshes and steep mountains all made transport across the countryside difficult.

➡️ Each of these harness bows would have sat on the back of a horse. The reins ran through the hole in the middle. The harness bows came from a grave in Mammen, Denmark.

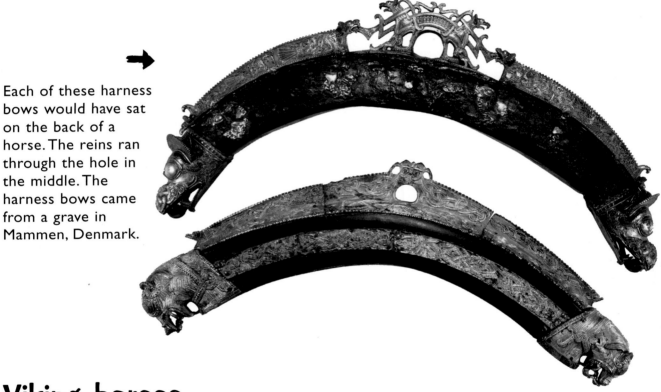

Viking horses

Whenever possible, the Vikings chose to travel by water. But if that wasn't possible, they had to go overland. People either walked or travelled on horseback. The Vikings were skilled riders, and we know that horses were important to the Vikings from the amount of horse equipment that has been found in graves. Wealthy Vikings were often buried with stirrups, bridles and harnesses. Sometimes they were even buried with their favourite horse. Horses were also used to carry goods, and to pull wagons and carts.

A wagon from the Oseberg ship burial.

A Viking Object

One of the objects buried in the Viking ship at Oseberg (see pages 26–7) was this wooden wagon. The wagon was probably pulled by two horses. The wagon is beautifully decorated with carvings. It is thought that such a highly decorated wagon was probably used in religious ceremonies.

Roads

Paths and roads tended to follow high ground wherever possible, to avoid bogs and dangerous river crossings. Where a route over marshy ground was unavoidable, the Vikings often built causeways out of wooden planks. In some places, bridges were built out of wood or stone across rivers. But in many places there were ferries, which could carry passengers across a fjord or a river.

Skiing and sledging

Overland travel could be easier during the winter months, when rivers and lakes froze over, and the land was covered in snow. The Vikings used skis, ice skates and sledges to travel across this icy landscape.

These horse bones were found at Jorvik. They were the right length for most human feet and were shaped to be used as skates.

Ice skates

The Vikings made skates out of bones to glide across ice. They often used horse or cattle bones. They drilled holes through the bones at either end and threaded leather thongs through the holes. They used the thongs to strap a bone beneath each foot. They made long wooden poles tipped with iron to push themselves along.

Skis

Viking skis were made from wood. Like the skates, they were attached to the foot with leather thongs threaded through holes. Sometimes people wore different-length skis on each foot – one long ski for gliding, and one short one covered with an animal skin for pushing themselves along. The Vikings usually used one stick to help them balance when they were skiing.

Sledges

Transporting cargo overland was often easier in the winter than in the summer. Large sledges loaded with goods were pulled by horses. The horses had iron spikes nailed into their hooves to stop them slipping on the snow and ice. Sledges could carry heavier loads than carts, and they did not get stuck like the wheels of a cart. It was also possible to take more direct routes in the winter, when rivers and lakes were frozen over.

A Viking Object

There were four wooden sledges buried in the Viking ship at Oseberg (see pages 26–7). This sledge has beautifully carved runners. On top is a box, attached to the frame with rope. The box is decorated with nail heads. This sledge was pulled by two horses.

➡

One of the sledges from the Oseberg ship burial.

Ship burials

When they died, the Vikings were buried with objects that they would need in the afterlife. For archaeologists today, these burial sites are a vital source of information about how the Vikings lived.

Oseberg and Gokstad

Seafaring was so important to the Vikings that wealthy people were often buried in ships. The buried ship was meant to carry the dead person to the next world, and it was filled with all the objects that he or she would need. Fine examples of such ships have been found at Oseberg and Gokstad, both in Norway, and in many other places too. In normal conditions wood gradually rots away, but both the Oseberg and the Gokstad ships were buried in thick, wet clay which had preserved the wooden ships.

This ship-shaped stone setting is around a grave on the Iron Age and Viking Age burial site of Lindholm Høje in Denmark.

Preserved remains

The excavations of the Gokstad and Oseberg ships gave archaeologists huge amounts of information about how Viking ships were made. At Oseberg, they also found lots of ship's equipment inside the ship, including a mast, a bucket for bailing out water, an anchor and oars. There were other objects too, including four sledges (see page 25), and a beautifully carved wagon. The remains of two female bodies were found in the burial. Archaeologists think that this burial may have been for a queen, who was probably buried with her slave.

The Oseberg ship was built in around 815–820 and sailed for many years before being buried in 834.

Harald Bluetooth
c.935 CE – c.985 CE

One of the most famous Viking burials is at Jelling in Denmark. This is not a ship burial, but two huge mounds which were erected in the 900s. It is thought that King Gorm and Queen Thyra, the parents of King Harald I of Denmark (also called Harald Bluetooth), were buried in Jelling. Harald brought Christianity to Denmark during his reign, and was for a short time also king of Norway. He erected a memorial stone at Jelling on which was carved: 'King Harald ordered this monument made in memory of Gorm, his father, and in memory of Thyra, his mother; that Harald who won for himself all of Denmark and Norway and made the Danes Christian.'

Timeline

CE

c.750s	Founding of Birka
793	Vikings raid monastery of Lindisfarne, Northumbria, England
794	Viking raids on the monasteries of Jarrow and Wearmouth in England
795	Vikings raid monastery of St Columba on Iona, Scotland
800s	Vikings settle the Orkney and Shetland Islands
c.800	Founding of Hedeby
815	Floki of Rogaland sets out from the Faroe Islands for Iceland
830s	Viking attacks on western Europe and Ireland begin
841	Vikings establish a *longphort* at Dubh-Linn (Dublin) in Ireland
843	Vikings plunder Nantes, France
844	First recorded Viking raid in Spain
845	Viking army attacks Paris
850	Viking fleet lands in Kent
859-62	Viking expedition into the Mediterranean Sea
860	Vikings attack Constantinople
865	Arrival of a large Viking army in England
866	York is captured by a Viking army
870s	Start of mass Viking settlement of Iceland
885–6	Vikings lay siege to Paris
911	Normandy becomes a Viking territory under King Rollo
c.982	Erik the Red sails to Greenland. Start of Viking settlements in Greenland
980s and 990s	New Viking attacks on England
991	Vikings defeat the English army at the Battle of Maldon
c.1000	Leif Eriksson sails to North America and names it Vinland
1016	Knut becomes King of England
1080s	Final unsuccessful Viking attacks bring the Viking Age to a close in England

Glossary

amber a type of fossilized resin

archaeological excavation a site that is carefully dug up and recorded by archaeologists

archaeologist a researcher who studies the remains of ancient peoples and civilisations

brocade Rich, woven fabric

Byzantine Empire The Eastern Roman Empire, centred on Constantinople (now Istanbul), that survived until 1453

cargo goods that are transported

colonizer someone who settles in a new country

colony a place under the control of another country and settled by people from that country

commerce trade

dugout a boat made out of a hollowed-out tree trunk

export to send goods to another country for sale

fjord a long and narrow sea inlet in a valley

fossilized describes an ancient plant or animal that has been turned into stone over millions of years

import to bring goods in from another country for sale

Islamic describes people who are members of the Muslim faith

knarr a Viking cargo ship

livestock animals such as cows, pigs or sheep

longship a Viking ship built for raiding and warfare

manoeuvre to move around

missionary someone who travels around in order to spread a particular religion

monastery a place where monks live and worship

Old Norse the language spoken by Scandinavians during the Viking Age

plunder to steal goods forcibly

prow the front of a ship

raider someone who makes a surprise attack and steals loot

rampart a defensive wall

rapid in a river, a place where the water flows very fast

resin a sticky substance that comes out of some trees

status describes rank or social standing

timber pieces of wood

whetstone a type of stone that can be used to sharpen knives

Index

Resources

History from Objects: The Vikings, Colin Malam, Wayland 2010

All about Ancient Peoples: The Vikings, Anita Ganeri, Watts, 2009

Men, Women and Children in Viking Times, Colin Hynson, Wayland, 2009

http://www.jorvik-viking-centre.co.uk/
Website of the Jorvik Viking Centre in York

http://www.bbc.co.uk/schools/primaryhistory/vikings/
BBC site for children about the Vikings

http://www.nmm.ac.uk/schools/resources/vikings-support-materials
Information and materials about the Vikings at the National Maritime
Museum's website